GLAMOURPUSS

THE ENCHANTING WORLD OF KITTY WIGS

by JULIE JACKSON

Photographs by JILL JOHNSON

CHRONICLE BOOKS

SAN FRANCISCO

All of the cats photographed in this book were adopted
or rescued. And, of course, none of them were harmed
during production.

We encourage you to adopt a kitty in need if you are able;
if not, please consider donating time or money to your
local no-kill animal shelter.

Library of Congress Cataloging-in-Publication Data
Jackson, Julie.
    Glamourpuss : the enchanting world of kitty wigs /
  by Julie Jackson ; photographs by Jill Johnson.
      p. cm.
    ISBN: 978-0-8118-6704-7
    1. Cats—Anecdotes. I. Title.

SF442.J34 2009
636.802'07—dc22
                        2008047228

Manufactured in China
Designed by Andrew Schapiro

10 9 8 7 6 5 4 3 2 1

Chronicle Books LLC
680 Second Street
San Francisco, California 94107

www.chroniclebooks.com

for **KAZ**

FOREWORD

by HEATHER ARMSTRONG
of DOOCE.COM

I'd like to imagine that the human tendency to anthropomorphize pets goes back to prehistoric times, specifically the scenario of a woman out gathering berries who stumbles across a den of baby lions and can't resist picking them up, scratching their bellies, and dressing them in elaborate gowns made from decorative foliage, right before the mama lion notices what is going on and makes her displeasure known. This would at least explain why I experience uncontrollable urges to dress my dogs in my daughter's clothing and why one of the most important questions my family asks itself each year is, "How much are we willing to spend on Halloween costumes for the dogs?" And every year the answer to that question is embarrassing.

I've made a modest living taking photographs of my two dogs Chuck and Coco dressed in various robes or shawls, and Chuck can often summon enough concentration to balance a beer bottle on top of his head. Both of them love this time we spend together because they are handsomely rewarded for their hard work, and in turn the fans of these photos get to join in on the fun of looking at a dog with a blender perched precariously between his ears.

Recently I took a set of photographs of Chuck, our male Super Mutt, in various seductive poses with a Kitty Wig on his head. And that is seemingly incongruous in so many ways, beginning with the fact that fitting his head into the wig was like trying to squeeze a whale through a keyhole. Also, Chuck's personality is not so much that of a seductive temptress as it is a moody and misunderstood prepubescent. But those photographs received by far the most response from fans, as if suddenly I had just given them what they hadn't known they'd been looking for all their lives: a picture of an animal in a ridiculous wig. Don't be surprised when you start to feel that same emotion when turning the pages in this book.

Holly Golightly:

"

HOW DO
I LOOK?

"

Paul Varjak:

"

I MUST SAY
I'M AMAZED.

"

—*Breakfast at Tiffany's*

If you've spent any time around a cat, you know they have much bigger things on their tiny minds than birds and squirrels. But what, exactly?

The daily distractions of being stuck in a feline body appear harmless enough to the average observer, but look closely: what is it our feline counterparts do most? To what activity do they devote more than 18 hours a day? Sleep. It's not like they're cleaning house or making a living, so it's never really seemed fair to me why they get to sleep so much while we tend to their worldly needs.

And how do we know if they're content? There's the occasional grateful head bonk or muffin-making episode, but why won't they speak to us? Just look at those pursed lips and squinty eyes. You and I both know they can talk—heck, they're probably fluent in Latin, the little skunks.

Your cat's not sleeping because she's tired. Sleep is an escape from her daily routine. Your cat is dreaming—dreaming of much bigger things than you or I will ever know. Armed only with an inanimate mouse toy or two, we're basically competing against our cats' naptime delusions of grandeur. No wonder they sleep all the time, and you can bet they'd roll their eyes at us if they could.

So here's my idea: Kitty Wigs: where feline desires and human imagination meet.

Kitty Wigs are a bridge into your cat's imagination. It's a chance for your cat to show you what it's really made of, and maybe even what it dreams about.

Why not introduce a glamorous hairstyle to spark your pet's imagination while you snap some photos? The world is overcrowded with insulting T-shirts and booties for dogs and fluffy collars with bells for cats that make them look like court jesters. Your fabulous feline is so much better than that, and you both know it.

Kitty Wigs are not only a way to add something sublime to your cat's character, but they provide a way for you to spend more quality time together—to dream together. It's an opportunity for you to show your cat new adventures, to show her that you understand her need to escape the dullness of everyday life and that you absolutely know she's worth much more than a pile of even the best cat toys money can buy.

While putting this book together, every time we tried a new wig on a familiar cat, we found they expressed much more than we could have imagined. The inner divas and demons are all there in the photos.

We think we're onto something. Imagine a line of Kitty Wig boutiques stretching from Dubai to Denver. Kitty Wigs take your relationship with your cat to another level, where every day is a new photo shoot.

THINK BIG.
THINK KITTY WIGS.

♡ Julie Jackson

"THEY'VE GOT TO REALIZE WE'RE MUCH MORE THAN JUST MODELS, UP HERE ON THE RUNWAY WORKING TWELVE-HOUR DAYS, LIVING ON SKINNY LATTES AND CHEWING GUM.

"SURE, THIS WIG MAKES ME A HOT NUMBER, BUT MY TUMMY'S STILL GROWLING. SO WHAT IF I TOOK A BITE OUT OF THOSE FLOWERS, WHO WILL NOTICE? THEY TASTE LIKE SALMON. TOTALLY WORTH IT."

Boone

"I KNEW IT WAS GOING TO BE ONE OF THOSE DAYS WHEN MY MEDS FELL INTO THE TOILET. NOW I CAN'T GET MY WIG ON STRAIGHT. BUT IT LOOKS OKAY, RIGHT?"

Fishstick

Orange Cat

"Note to self: Paris during Fashion Week is always too exhausting. Next year, stay home and buy magazines instead."

"SOMETIMES I'VE GOT TO BE SOMEONE ELSE FOR A WHILE. AFTER A TOUGH DAY OF BORING MEET-INGS AND WHINY CLIENTS, THERE'S NOTHING BETTER THAN DONNING THE BLUE BEAUTY AND HITTING MY FAVORITE DIVE."

Bacon

"PINK,

SHE EEZ ZE COLOUR DU JOUR, NON?

TRÈS CHIC,
TRÈS CHANEL,
TRÈS BELLE!

After a long day at Salon le Mew, le carpet—
how you say?—she matches le drapes.

C'EST MAGNIFIQUE!"

Chicken

Tugboat

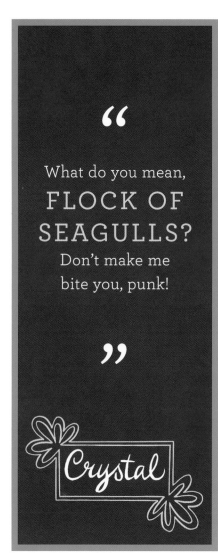

"

What do you mean,

FLOCK OF
SEAGULLS?

Don't make me
bite you, punk!

"

Crystal

"**I LIKE TO KEEP MY LOOK FRESH AND YOUNG,** SO I WEAR THE CLASSIC SHADE OF RED THAT MADE ME FAMOUS. IT ALWAYS GIVES ME A THRILL TO MEET THE NEW GENERATION OF KIDS. **AFTER ALL, I'M THE ORIGINAL COUGAR!**"

Boone

Chicken

"I am one **FINGER-SNAPPIN'**, **BONGO-TAPPIN'**, **MIDNIGHT RAPPIN'**, **FRESH-CREAM LAPPIN'** *cooool daddy-o.*"

Fern

"SINCE I LAUNCHED MY TABBYGIRL LINE OF COSMETICS, I'VE BEEN TRAVELING NON-STOP. WE JUST GOT BACK FROM DUBAI AND NEXT WE'RE GOING TO ICELAND. KITTIES ALL OVER THE WORLD ARE INTERESTED IN LOOKING AND FEELING THEIR BEST, AND NOTHING CAN RAMP UP YOUR CONFIDENCE LIKE A KITTY WIG. THE ONE I'M WEARING NOW IS MY FAVORITE SHADE OF AUBERGINE—IT MAKES ME FEEL FIERCE AND IN CONTROL."

"HI! YOU'RE HOME! DID YOU HAVE A HARD DAY? CAN I FIX YOU A CATNIP MOJITO? HOW DO YOU LIKE MY SEXY NEW HAIRSTYLE?"

"I really prefer living in Phoenix because the weather's so mild here and the Houston humidity was doing nothing for my hair."

Hercules

"NYAH-NYAH BABY! STICK YOUR HEAD IN GRAVY, WRAP IT UP IN BUBBLE GUM AND SEND IT TO THE NAVY!"

Lyla

Sam

"I love outdoor concerts because there's always lots of fresh green grass to nibble on. Keeps me from having beer breath!" (*burp*)

"OH, WOW, IT'S DEFINITELY KICK-ING IN NOW, I'M REALLY FEELIN' IT! STOP THE CAR, I'M PEAKIN'!"

Earl

RESIDENT JOYOLOGIST.

"BLONDE SETS OFF MY BEAUTIFUL EYES AND I THINK IT MAKES ME LOOK TAN, DON'T YOU? NOW ALL I NEED IS A PLANE TICKET, A BIKINI, AND A SWEDISH ACCENT."

Fern

"CAN YOU HEAR THE DRUMS, FERNANDO?"

Boone

"ACTUALLY, I MADE THIS WIG WITH LEFTOVER MACRAMÉ FROM THE SEVENTIES!

"REDUCE, REUSE, RECYCLE, BABY!"

Gravy

Boone

"Oh hey—what's up? The wig? Vintage sixties. I picked it up in Amsterdam when I was hanging out with Niko and the Underground. I feel like I'm back at the Factory making movies and trading clothes with Viva. Seems like only yesterday."

"There are never enough hours in the days of a queen, and her nights have too many."

"Look at them putting shoes on that dog. How pathetically ridiculous!"

Boone

"Yeah, I know, ever since that new **IKEA** opened, **WE'VE JUST BEEN GOING MAD!** Who knew they made cat beds? **I FEEL SO . . . SWEDISH!**"

"**OH MAAAAN,** I'm just hanging out, Officer. I guess I left my collar and tags at home, but you can call my owners—they know I'm here. This is just lemonade, and that bird was totally dead when I found it. Whaddya mean, 'Get a haircut'? This is a wig, dude! **YOU'RE HARSHIN' MY NATURE BUZZ!**"

Flash

"I'll try anything once, twice if I like it! But this red is here to stay. You wouldn't believe all the attention I've been getting. Maybe I'll get another tattoo. No one needs to know I'm from Hoboken."

Apollo

Mature feline seeks tomcat companion for weekend matinees and midnight snacks.

NO FISHY BUSINESS.

"

I WOULDN'T
RECOMMEND
INSANITY
to just anyone, but
IT'S ALWAYS
WORKED
for me.

"

Gravy

"SWEETIE, YOU'VE GOT MY SYMPATHY, BUT I HAVE *NO* IDEA HOW TO MAKE TEA."

Gravy

"YES, HONEY, IT'S CATNIP CAKE. PROMISE ME YOU WON'T ROLL YOUR HEAD IN IT BEFORE THE PARTY STARTS. *PLEASE?*"

"When will they **STOP TRYING TO IMPRESS ME** with these **BIRFDAY PARTIES** and just let me sleep?"

Skittles

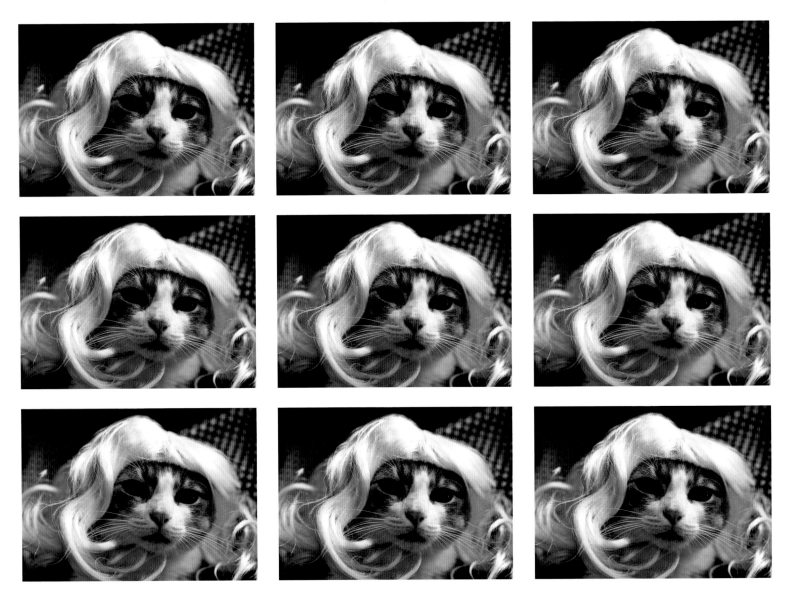

"Honey, if I had a nickel for every no-good man who's come through here . . . more coffee, sweetie? Save your fork, there's pie!"

Mona

"

INNOCENCE IS MY MIDDLE NAME.

NO, REALLY, IT IS—

my parents were

very optimistic.

WOULD I LIE TO YOU?

"

Romeo

"SCREWED UP EYES.
SCREWED DOWN
HAIRDO. I FEEL LIKE A
SPIDER FROM MARS."

OOPS,
you caught me!
**MY CRAZINESS FOR
CRAFTS IS
COMPLETELY OUT
OF CONTROL!**
Who knows what I'll
make next—
besides a big mess!

Romeo

"

I AM STRONG,
I AM INVINCIBLE,

I AM
KIT-TAY!

Mrooowww!

"

Red

"AND NOW I'D LIKE TO SLOW IT DOWN WITH A SPECIAL LITTLE NUMBER I CALL 'SPOTLIGHT SERENADE.'"

"WHY, IT WAS EASY PICKIN' OUT MY WIG COLOR—IT AIN'T FANCY, I JUST WANTED SOMETHIN' TO MATCH MY PAWS. NOTHIN' HIGH-FALUTIN', BUT IT SURE CAN MAKE ME FEEL LIKE THE BELLE OF THE BARN DANCE."

"I DON'T REALLY CARE WHAT YOU THINK, BABY; **IT'S MY HAIR AND MY DECISION.** BESIDES, I DON'T HAVE TO LICK IT FOR WEEKS, IT JUST STAYS THIS WAY. LIKE MAGIC. **GOD, YOU'RE BORING.** WHAT'S SO FUNNY?"

Mitchell

Bogie

"I was thrilled to land the leading role in *The Taming of the Shrew*. I'm totally channeling Liz Taylor, can't you tell?"

I WANT TO BE
MISS FANCY PAWS USA
because I love to travel and
teach children sign language.

MY
FAVORITE
COLOR
IS PINK

and my pet cause is world peace.

Rooster

"THIS PARTY IS THE DEFINITION OF CUTE OVERLOAD. I FEEL A LITTLE SICK TO MY TUMMY. I MIGHT BARF RAINBOWS."

Skittles

The narcoleptic babysitter: "Nuh-uh, little mister, I've got my eye on you and I'm gonna tell your parents what a bad little boy you were and . . . zzzzzzz. . . ."

"Cool cat in hot wig.
This color matches my eyes.
Last thing mouse will see.

And who said cats couldn't
master the art of haiku? Sheesh!"

Mitchell

"CAN YOU BELIEVE LIV TYLER GOT THE PART OF ARWEN IN *LORD OF THE RINGS*? THAT ROLE WAS MINE, MINE, MINE!"

"LA-LA-LA-LA! I CAN'T HEAR YOU!"

Shaft

Bogie

"FOR YOUR INFORMATION, I ALMOST WON AN EMMY— TWICE! SO LET'S JUST DO ANOTHER TAKE AND GET IT RIGHT THIS TIME."

THE MODELS

Apollo

Apollo is a sociable cat who is often mistaken for David Bowie when bewigged. He loves people and other animals—he was even caught out one night dining with a raccoon. Apollo has such a regal face that his parents are convinced he's a direct descendant of King Tut's pet pumas.

Bacon

Bacon's mom Kaz claims he's the most famous bar cat in the world. When he's not behind the bar at Lee Harvey's in Dallas (where "bacon—not the cat" is on the menu), he's usually snacking on Meow Mix, napping, running through sprinklers, or posing for wig shoots. Bacon's favorite song is "Girlfriend Is Better" by the Talking Heads.

Bibi

Bibi is one classy and sassy dame. She prances around regally as if she rules the universe. Her dream has always been to be a model, and she loves being the center of attention. She also loves to play with mom's cosmetics and often ends up a hot mess covered in powder. But in her eyes she is Princess Bibi, ruler of all.

Boone

Boone's favorite spot is between Julie and her keyboard, where he makes vigorous edits with his powerfully cruel tail. He has been known to pass out suddenly while trying to pay attention, which has made him an Internet sensation (search on Google for "narcoleptic cat" to see his video). Boone enjoys triple-cream cheeses, samba music, and Bollywood soundtracks.

Bogie

Don't tell anyone, but Bogie's mom says that his best friend is a 90-pound yellow Lab. He loves company so much that he even runs when the doorbell rings (luckily he can't answer the phone!). He's a fabulous and attentive host, and he's only three years old.

Chicken

Chicken was rescued from an abandoned house along with his sister Rooster. He loves a nice shot of Grey Goose in the morning, taking a long roll in the dirt, and then cleaning himself for hours in front of the mirror (just like his dad). A cat with discerning tastes, Chicken knows that toilet water is the best, and his favorite vacation spot? Michael Jackson's Neverland Ranch.

Crystal

Crystal is a party girl who would be perfect in a feline remake of *Breakfast at Tiffany's*. She's a retro kind of cat who loves listening to her dad's records of 40s and 50s swing music. When she's not basking in the sun enjoying a life of leisure, Crystal is probably scoping out the neighborhood and visiting friends across the street.

Fern

Fern was born in an East Dallas alley, then showed up on her mom's back porch one day to be adopted. She's a svelte 7 pounds with a high-pitch meow and a stinging bite that has brought tears to a grown man's eye. Fern loves tree houses, flannel sheets, and dog beds. Her favorite song is "Saturday in the Park" by Chicago.

Earl

After surviving a five-story plunge to a concrete patio in the summer of 2000, Earl decided to throw caution to the wind and explore his inner style diva. He soon developed a penchant for the peculiar—maybe it was the kitty morphine? Earl has resided in Baltimore, Brooklyn, Marrakesh, Taipei, Dubai, and now Dallas. Next stop: Southfork.

Fishstick

Fishstick is a yam-shaped calico girl who enjoys trapping flies with her paw, standing on them, and promptly forgetting about them; rolling BBs around at 4:00 AM; and staring at things no one else sees. When not playing a brisk game of "Made You Look," Fishstick can usually be found swaying to "South American Way" a la Carmen Miranda.

Flash

Flash was found with her siblings in a box abandoned on the side of the road in Rockland, Maine. She loves fetching, snuggling, wet food, tree houses, and squirrel stalking. Flash's favorite song is "Snowbird" by Anne Murray.

Hercules

Hercules is a former stray who was discovered in the parking lot of a Mexican restaurant. He's a furry ball of sunshine who likes to be the center of attention at all times. He even taught himself to use the toilet without any training, and secretly enjoys making humans wait in line at the bathroom door.

Gravy

Sexy and versatile, Gravy is a Libra who has already appeared in a fashion shoot for *Vogue* (October 2003). He enjoys running on the beach without his shirt, being handfed goldfish (the cracker kind), practicing the art of massage, and showing off his green eyes to the ladies. Gravy is a genuine playboy and a talker when the lights go out. He digs "Love Train" by the O'Jays.

Lyla

Lyla is a very playful kitten who loves to bug her big brother Sam. Her favorite toy is whatever happens to cross her path at any moment. She loves to sleep in her kitty carrier, but she's usually playing too madly to sleep. Her favorite band is Black Tie Dynasty, and her favorite photographer is Jill Johnson. Lyla is a princess who can never get enough attention.

Matteo

Matteo is a very cool cat with a preference for white meat, particularly turkey. He's a quiet boy who never loses his composure and is always available for an afternoon of movies and lounging on the sofa. Matteo is very friendly to guests and hardly ever whines.

Mona

Mona ("monkey" in Spanish) is a double-jointed girl who once spent three days in a tree and had to be rescued by a higher power. She loves flamenco music and wishes she could spend her days in Havana eating her favorite dish of roasted chicken with baked carrots and drinking Cuba Libres.

Mitchell

Mitchell is an 8-year-old, 18-pound furry ball of self-important love. He enjoys the music of Bob Marley and bullying his sister, Maggie. He loves his food and always asks for dessert. Mitchell has a black belt in fly-catching and does some of his best thinking under the shed in the backyard.

Orange Cat

Orange Cat is an orange cat who regularly walks right into neighbors' houses to socialize and check for treats. Even though he's about 15 years old, he still thinks he's a dog: he comes running when whistled for and enjoys a good pat on the head.

Red

Red is too young to drink but often tries to sneak a sip of any unattended cocktail. He enjoys hanging out on the roof with his buddies and likes finely chopped beef tenderloin au jus. His favorite song is "Born to Run" by Bruce Springsteen.

Rooster

Rooster was rescued along with her brother, Chicken, who she thinks is a bully. She loves creamer in the morning and showing off the long fur that grows between her paws. Rooster loves to dress up like a dog and walk with her dog buddies Lux and Chi Chi around the neighborhood. Her favorite song is "Two Doors Down" by her hero, Dolly Parton.

Romeo

Romeo will often reach out to people, put his paws up to their bodies, and hug them—he's a cuddly lover like his namesake. He is very frisky, loves to play, and makes a game out of almost everything. Still a spastic kitten, sometimes Romeo freaks out and runs all over the house channeling that famous mongoose, Rikki-Tikki-Tavi.

Sam

Sam is a very laid-back cat who loves the outdoors almost as much as he loves his mama. His luck changed for the better when he was adopted on New Year's Eve 2007. Don't tell anyone, but his favorite toy is called "Blue," and nobody better mess with it.

Shaft

The beautiful Shaft (John Shaft) was rescued from a grocery store parking lot. Don't be fooled by his smooth moves, he's a bad mother—shut yo' mouth!

Tugboat

Tugboat's goal is to be the first kitten to win a gold medal in rhythmic gymnastics and she is committed to competing in the 2012 games. She loves anything attached to a stick with string, leaping in the air, swatting at feathers, and acing graceful landings. A huge fan of Bessie Smith, her favorite tune is "Give Me a Pigfoot and a Bottle of Beer."

Skittles

Skittles is a calico kitten that was rescued from a pound. She lives in a house full of animals including dogs, cats, lizards, and bunnies, so she's a little confused and thinks she must be a dog. She acts accordingly, eats dog food, and can frequently be found singing her favorite song, "Who Let the Dogs Out?" (Hint: it was someone quite calico.)

JULIE THANKS:

Kate Woodrow, Christina Loff, and Andrew Schapiro at Chronicle, for making this dream come true. Sarah Sockit, for guidance and being such a tenacious agent.

Jill Johnson, for falling from the sky into my life and performing miracles. Chris Jackson, for furthering my insanity and keeping us in cocktails so stylishly. Stitchy McYarnpants, for bringing the funny when I was running out of steam.

Heather Armstrong, for the foreword and her amazing daily photos of Chuck at dooce.com.

Allison and Jessica, for your love and support, without which we might never have left the ground.

To Kaz, for being a steadfast friend these 20+ years and the most generous animal lover I know. Wendy and Shannon for their help with endless cat-wrangling. Amy for gluing Jill's eyelashes together. L.K. Peterson for the clever kitty haiku.

To everyone who has shared their photos with the Kitty Wigs Flickr group and my beloved Kitty Wigs e-news subscribers—you're the best!

To the early enthusiasts: Meg at Cute Overload; Stacey and Yoshi; Heather, Derek, Chieka, Bug and Spoo; Myla, Daisy and Bear; EllenJo, Floyd, Ivan (& Harrison, too); Jim, Jasper and Chuy; Molly and her crazy bunch.

To my family and friends for their endless love and encouragement.

To Rhydon for driving across the country to bring us the gift of Boone.

To pets throughout the years who have brightened my life so much: Sam, Tiger, Chelsie, Anonymous Bob, Ben, Miss Kitty, Tip & Trixie, Nell, Basil, Othello, Gay & Lusty, Boone, and the littlest Jackson, Tito.

JILL THANKS:

Julie Jackson in all her glory! For her trust, fun-loving support, and generosity, shine on you crazy diamond! Kate Woodrow at Chronicle Books and the talented Sarah Sockit. You girls rock! Jeff Guinn and Jim Donovan for their book guidance, wisdom and time. Kaz, our official cat wrangler, you are a life saver. Wendy and Shannon, you get the award for most enthusiasm and best cat stylin' (you too Tony!).

Chris Jackson and his magical Bloody Marys, where are my red flip flops? My best sidekick and kitty show assistant Sara Kline, you are my memory. Allie for all your photo inspiration and for mailing me the pink and blue wig that made Chicken famous. Amy for taking pics of us on a wild night and driving me around and around the Dallas highways, Nacho Average Pal.

To my sweet golden family, Brian, Lux, Chi Chi, Rooster, and Chicken. After many fun years with his family and furry friends,

Chicken passed away in October 2008. We all miss his beauty, grace, and biscuit making every day.

Mama, you are my rock and biggest supporter. I love you till the numbers stop. Thanks for always believing in me no matter how silly or strange.

To all my family for their love and acceptance of my insanity: Daddy, J.B., Ash, Matt, Curtis, Andrew, and Jen.

To Nana, my true sweetheart and light, you are my sunshine!

To Betty Johnson who instilled in me a love and delight in all creatures furry.

Most of all to those caring, sweet spirits who rescue and save cats and dogs around the world! You are loved!

JULIE AND JILL BOTH THANK:

All the wonderful kitty parents who gave their time and shared their precious protégés: Kari, Nancy, Kaz, Wendy & Shannon, A'dina, Kara, Allison, Jim, Stephanie, Ashley, Ann, Kim, Brenda, Leanne, Colleen, B.Z., and Jo Dufo.

We dedicate this book to Chicken, the very embodiment of Kitty Wigs. He had to move on before we went to print, but he left this tremendous legacy. Rest in peace, Chicken. May you always have kitty wings.

Julie Jackson is the creator of Kitty Wigs and www.kittywigs.com, where she sells upscale hairpieces for special felines. Kitty Wigs has been featured in fashion layouts for *Harper's Bazaar* Japan and *CosmoGirl*, in *Business Week*, and on CNN's *Anderson Cooper 360°* and BBC's *Graham Norton*. Julie is also the force behind Subversive Cross Stitch, a modern craft meme that updates old-fashioned samplers with snarky sentiments.

Jill Johnson is a freelance photographer specializing in portraits and photojournalism. A wild adventurer with deep roots in Texas, she loves all creatures madly. Jill lives with her husband and furry family: Lux, Chi Chi, and Rooster. See more of her work at www.jilljohnsonphoto.com.

There's always more to see at kittywigs.com: photo shoot outtakes, stories from the photographer, tips on how to get your cat to cooperate, latest press and news, and, of course, wigs to buy!

We encourage you to share photos of your kitty in a wig at www.flickr.com/groups/kittywigs